It Is
What
It Is!

NOW
WHAT?

A GUIDE TO SELF-MOTIVATION
AND EFFECTIVE TEAM LEADERSHIP

SUZANNE SLOVAK

Cover design: Kristina Edstrom

PEAK PRESS

An Imprint for GracePoint Publishing (www.GracePointPublishing.com)

GracePoint Matrix, LLC
624 S. Cascade Ave Suite 201
Colorado Springs, CO 80903
www.GracePointMatrix.com
Email: Admin@GracePointMatrix.com

SAN # 991-6032

A Library of Congress Control Number has been requested and is pending.

ISBN: (Paperback) 978-1-966346-20-3
eISBN: 978-1-966346-21-0

Books may be purchased for educational, business, or sales promotional use.
For bulk order requests and price schedule contact:
Orders@GracePointPublishing.com
Printed in U.S.A

Table of Contents

Preface

It Is What It Is

Hello, I'm Suzanne, a seasoned voyager with an impressive thirty-five-plus-year odyssey through the ever-evolving world of the printing industry. With over fifteen years of proficiency in the art of management, I have these skills under my creative belt, leading me on a whirlwind journey that's had all the excitement of a Shakespearean drama, but thankfully without the tragic endings.

This incredible journey commenced during my formative years, as I immersed myself in the inner workings of my family's cherished photography studio. This establishment, a labor of love, was overseen by my mother, who orchestrated its operations with care and dedication. The images were expertly captured through my father's lens, while my brother and two skillful photographers added their talents to the mix. I had two jobs: One was to help print the wedding albums and the other was to be the primary videographer. Our collaborative efforts resulted in a symphony of small business mechanics that produced beautiful visual memories and taught me priceless lessons in efficiency and the irreplaceable value of seamless teamwork.

Within the tapestry of my journey, one pivotal chapter placed me at the helm of a graphics company, a venture that brought together around fifteen individuals. This experience sharpened my ability to steer the course of a thriving enterprise and became a teaching period in the art of managing not just myself but also a diverse team. Navigating the intricacies of this dynamic environment, I cultivated a profound understanding of leadership dynamics, collaboration, and the delicate balance between fostering individual growth and guiding collective achievements.

Zooming ahead to the present day, I'm still that same wide-eyed youngster, but now I am armed with a grown-up mission. Picture me, brimming with enthusiasm, as I witness those around me moving at a pace no faster than a snail's while they have the potential to dash like cheetahs. And that's when it struck me. How we can rouse these individuals, unveiling the secrets to revving up their professional drive and turbocharging their creativity?

Now, let's weave in a new twist: a reminder of the story of the Pied Piper from our youth. Imagine the man of legend, but this time as a villain, stealthily pilfering productivity and time from unsuspecting businesses. As we embark on this journey together, please think of me as your guide, ready to thwart this modern-day pied piper and his tactics that drain productivity and diminish success.

So, here's the grand strategy: We're on the brink of unearthing a treasure trove of my extensive experiences, along with some fascinating people from history and everyday folks, peppered with playful anecdotes and my distinct charm. Prepare for the revelation of strategies that elevate businesses to harmonious heights. This book is designed to both entertain and empower.

Buckle up, for this isn't your typical business guide. It's your backstage pass to a symphony of triumphs, complete with front row seats. Let's conquer the pied piper of lost productivity and usher in an era of unparalleled accomplishment!

Introduction

It Is What It Is

At the beginning of the new millennium, I managed a graphics company. In this role, I was confronted with different personalities and communication styles. Fortunately for me, this has always fascinated me. I was not ready for an attitude expressed by a pop culture phrase: *It is what it is.*

This phrase was not new to me, but it never affected me quite like this until I was a manager. At first, it amused me, but then it frustrated me. I had seen its turbulent actions move like wildfire, jumping from person to person. I caught a glimpse of it a few years ago when a new, younger employee joined the team. As he began singing a simple melody, more and more employees joined. To some employees, it gave them a feeling of calm, maybe even a sense of liberation, but I felt a broad spectrum of emotions from hopelessness to anger.

The truth behind the Pied Piper fairy tale is that it is *not* a fairy tale. There are accounts that say it is based on historical facts dating back to 1284 in Hamelin, Germany. The original story speaks nothing of rats. This was the embellishment of Robert Browning, meant to teach the importance of honoring agreements. According to various searches, in 1384, the village of Hamelin's records stated that it had been one-hundred years since the children left; there was a manuscript from 1440 that survived and described an event where a piper clothed in many colors had led 130 children born in the town of Hamelin away; and there are some references to a depiction of the infamous Pied Piper in stained glass in a Hamelin church from 1284, but that was destroyed in 1660. Nonetheless, the metaphor of a pied piper is the same: It is a person who offers strong but delusive enticement, who makes irresponsible promises, or a charismatic person who attracts followers, often to no good end.

Managing a graphics company introduced me to an array of colorful personalities and communication styles. This intricate web of human interaction has always intrigued me, offering a fascinating lens through which to view the dynamics of teamwork. Yet, the particular cultural catchphrase "it is what it is" managed to cast a shadow over this otherwise captivating landscape.

While not an unfamiliar phrase, its impact resonated profoundly as I navigated my managerial responsibilities. Initially, it elicited chuckles, but soon, its influence morphed into a source of frustration as its nonchalant spread gained momentum. What started as an innocuous utterance soon revealed its sinister nature, spreading from one individual to another. I distinctly recall encountering its eerie influence when a fresh-faced, new employee introduced it to the workplace.

The modern pied piper's song held a chilling power capable of halting productivity, suffocating creativity, and extinguishing motivation. While seemingly harmless, this phrase served as a harbinger of complacency, an acceptance of the status quo that snuffed out the fires of progress and innovation.

In the infamous story of yore, on the day the children went missing, the street they are believed to have last been seen on is referred to as the street without drums because no one is allowed to play music or dance there. What happened to the children is still a mystery. Historians have several theories, from the children being uprooted to emigrating to a better life to the plague, or even to a children's crusade. Whatever happened, it is evident that the children were lost to their parents.

The person in history wearing this brightly colored—*pied*—coat is a frame of mind in today's world. The statement "it is what it is" is a pretext or a reason to justify a course of action that is not the *real* reason. Or, in a layperson's terms, it is a cop-out, an excuse not to pursue the matter any further.

You may have picked up this book for one of two reasons: Maybe you are tired of employees following the lead of others who lack true direction, and you're looking for advice to help lead them to discover their full potential, or perhaps you want to develop your own unrealized capabilities while avoiding the lull of complacency.

Here is the story of my crusade to bring back productivity, inspire creativity, and actively foster motivation in others when I grew tired of losing colleagues. I refuse to look around and say, "It is what it is."

This book will light a fire so that we can find our way forward. This book's pages unfold my narrative, a journey ignited within me when I reached a breaking point, witnessing my colleagues succumb to the mesmerizing tune of pied pipers, one where I refused to accept or repeat their utterances

Above all, this book serves as the beacon that will rekindle the flames of passion within us. Its purpose is to guide us back to the realms of creativity and productivity, to breathe life into our motivation, and to rally those around us. It aims to reignite the vibrant spirit within companies and individuals alike, enabling us to thrive again.

Chapter One

The Pied Piper

It Is What It Is

The book you are reading is the story of my journey of recognizing a toxic culture phrase that invaded our homes and our workforce and what I did to navigate and course correct. I first became aware of this phrase in the '90s. Back then, we had a new hire in his early twenties.

These words flowed from him effortlessly, akin to a gentle, unassuming melody. It was as if he possessed a mystical ability to summon this phrase with ease. I stood witness as he serenaded our manager with this peculiar song. The manager's initial reaction was one of slight retreat, a subtle step back, his demeanor tinged with surprise, almost as though he had stumbled upon an unexpected presence in the air. And there it hung, those five simple words as if suspended in time.

Yet, what unfolded next was even more fascinating. The young man's lips curved into a Grinch-like knowing smile as if he held a secret connection to some otherworldly realm. With an almost whimsical dance in his step, he would spin away, vanishing into what seemed like an enchanted realm of his creation and leaving his managers forlorn and baffled.

Soon, this siren song cast its spell over the other employees. One by one, department by department, they joined the chorus, *it is what it is*, when their work was questioned or their deadlines missed. They would smile, shrug their shoulders, and dance off to their enchanted lands without a backward glance. The manager, befuddled with how to handle the increasing number of employees expressing the same song, succumbed over time and joined the ranks of nonchalance.

In short order, the lilting melody began to weave its enchantment over the other employees. An inexorable transformation unfolded, akin to falling dominoes one into the next and toppling into the next department, and then the next, pulling managers in one by one until the effect wiped the owner along as well. They all joined the harmonious chorus, their voices melding seamlessly with the refrain as if glancing back with derision as we watched. The dancing shoulders shrugged, and smiles were exchanged, all veiled beneath the weight of resigned acceptance, and carried them off to their private realms of enchantment.

As each of my fellow employees started to embrace the song, more things went through pro-duction incorrectly. Projects began to go in the trash because they were unacceptable, and some were sent to the clients only to be kicked back because they were wrong. Those clients were unhappy, and some took their work elsewhere. The song of the pied piper was turning people into goof-offs. The coordinators who wrote up the work orders for the jobs stopped checking what they gave the computer people. The computer people admitted they saw the mistakes but sent the orders along anyway. The printers commented that all they were supposed to do is print what the computer people give them, so the orders went down the line. Some employees would see a mistake, but none stopped and questioned it or had it corrected, because no one felt invested; no one cared.

Depending on what was in a project, I may not have even seen it to be able to stop it from getting out to the customer, or by the time a project got to me, and I put the brakes on it, there had been a lot of time and materials wasted. It seemed that in all the steps of the process, everyone turned a blind eye to poor quality and mistakes. This was apparent in other ways as well.

I saw how this had spread beyond production when I noticed a group of five employees leaving the premises together for an hour lunch, and upon return, one of them clocked them all out. They then sat and talked in the lunchroom for up to a half hour before each clocking back in, pretending as though they hadn't also taken an hour for lunch. While the time card may have indicated their lunch was only thirty minutes, they were stealing more than an hour daily. Think about the person hours this robs from a business! In a small company of about twenty-five people, these five employees doing this five times a week, every week, added to a significant loss of money. Some of you may think I resent them getting away with making easy money, but I look at it from the business owner's perspective because of my family's business. Having grown up with my mother and father running a small wedding studio, I understood firsthand how crucial money management is in a small business. When all the bills are paid at the end of the day, if nothing remains for raises or bonuses, you don't get them!

I distinctly recall conversing with their manager, addressing the concerning pattern of incomplete project follow-through and the imperative to encourage a culture of constructive feedback. We delved into the issue of diminishing work quality and the repercussions it posed. It became evident that the manager was also aware of the lunchtime discussions—the sessions where the enchanting refrain originated.

We talked about the gravity of the situation and the gradual erosion of our client base, serving as a tangible manifestation of our troubles. Astonishingly, the manager appeared to concur with every observation and insight I made. They agreed but were either unwilling or unable to exact any change. Here's where my astonishment deepened as I found my own words echoed: *It is what it is.*

My reaction oscillated between disbelief and exasperation. Here was a situation demanding action, a circumstance warranting vigilance, yet the response appeared to be a passive surrender to fate. At this moment, my role seemed inconsequential, that of a mere worker bee navigating within a hive once teeming with industriousness, now teetering on the precipice of disarray. The urgency I felt clashed with this complacent acceptance, leaving me both frustrated and bewildered.

It seemed that nothing I could do would change the work environment, and it started to affect my mental health. I could not make a change for the company's betterment, and my stress level was off the chart. I also could not do the work of all the employees within the chain of productivity. Because of that, I knew I couldn't thrive in the environment that had settled into my workplace. It was time to find another hive. As luck would have it, a company I knew of came calling. They were going through a reorganization and becoming a large format print company. They needed a manager and asked if I would take on the job. I said yes! That is when I took that hypnotic seducement and asked myself, *Now what?* I realized that for me it was time to move on.

The company was moving to a new location, and I would manage and oversee the setup of the new facility. All was going smoothly: walls were being painted, workspaces laid out, and the latest equipment came in off the trucks. The building was swarming with enthusiasm. Anything and everything felt possible and exciting. The company was bringing in new clients, and work was going out the door. We hired more people to help with the influx of work. We added more equipment to keep up with the demand. We were even adding new equipment that would broaden our production line. It was an exciting time for everyone at the company. This hive was buzzing.

Then, one day, I heard that old whisper. I thought I had left it far behind, but I was wrong. He looked different from the one I saw years ago, but it was the same old number. A new pied piper had called me to his workstation. It started light and snappy.

"Hey!" The tune went. "This didn't work."

On an upbeat, I asked, "What is the issue?"

He replied, "It's not right. Something is wrong."

"Okay," I said. "What is it?"

"It's not working. Here you go." He handed me the project, and with a smile, he belted out the chorus, "It is what it is!"

He seemed to twirl before me, swinging and swaying as he danced away.

I stood there still, holding the paperwork in my hands. I was motionless as I watched him sashay down the hall to the time clock on the wall and punch out for an early lunch. It was a minute or two before I came back to my senses. I remember wondering, *What just happened? Is he going to fix it, or was this his way of saying he didn't know how to fix it? Did he just imply that it's my problem, not his?*

14

The song had been sung and even broadcast through the office. More and more employees picked up on the catchy tune as they sang along, turning the entire office into a disorganized glee club. One by one, as problems arose on projects, employees would shrug it off, pass it along, and recite the incantation, luring the next one to join in. What made matters worse was that the owners asked me to make the projects work, but that was not always possible. If I couldn't fix the oversights of their not reading a work order, not paying attention to what they were doing, or worse, just not caring, then prints and materials would go in the trash.

One young man told me he didn't care about the project going in the trash: "It's not my money after all."

I remember dropping my head, taking a deep, slow breath, and simply explaining to him the significant labor cost.

"That $900 worth of acrylic that just went in the dumpster, not including the wasted time and other materials needed to redo the job, is *your* money."

He asked me, "How is it *my* money?"

I replied, "If the company is not making a profit or has to keep charging more for jobs unnecessarily needing to be redone, do you think you will get that raise or even keep your job if the company sees you as a liability due to increasing losses?"

That quieted things for a time, but the more the owners asked me to fix the slipups in order to stay profitable, the harder it was for me to keep up. It seemed I couldn't motivate and inspire the employees to step up or to care more for their part in the process. As I would find something incorrect at the beginning of the manufacturing process, I would ask the operator to fix the problems before printing it. I sometimes got the response of, "I can fix it if you really want me to."

I found myself at my wits' end. Of course I wanted the operator to fix it! That's why I returned the work order to the technician to fix the problems before they were printed, saving precious time and money and keeping the project out of the trash. After all, that is the goal of any good company that wishes to succeed.

The owners were fostering a concerning trend, leaning on me, the manager, to salvage projects whenever employees fell short. It was like a grim rendition of the old saying: "If you want something done right, do it yourself." Instead of tackling the core issue, they passed the buck to me to rectify it. There were no repercussions for employees who shirked responsibility for their work. The owners were wary of upsetting the workforce, with just about fifteen people in the company, afraid of what would happen if they suddenly cracked down.

They even restrained me from holding employees accountable, preferring to avoid confrontation instead. It became more convenient for them to delegate the task of fixing mistakes to me rather than addressing them head on. This approach flew in the face of the wisdom encapsulated in the old Chinese proverb, "give a man a fish, and he will eat for a day; teach a man to fish, and you feed him for a lifetime." If only the owners had encouraged employees to step up, think critically, take pride in their work, and collaborate as a team, everyone would have flourished.

Instead, I began to examine the influence of this collective belief on the employees. I observed how they were all heading down a path of apathy, convincing themselves that not caring, not thinking, and not trying were synonymous with working smarter, not harder. This belief blinded the workers to the reality of leading a fulfilling and prosperous life.

I witnessed how this complacent axiom lured them down a road of detachment, persuading them that indifference, lack of engagement, and minimal effort were all okay. The mesmerizing melody veiled their perception of what it truly meant to lead a rewarding and prosperous existence. So, amid this alluring chorus, why did I remain steadfast, refusing to yield?

Rather than being lured into this enticement, I was drawn to examine its effects on my colleagues. In this exploration, I observed how this enchanting melody guided them down a treacherous path. On this path, apathy and indifference reigned supreme, masquerading as what they believed exhibited the practice of working smarter rather than harder. Yet, as our conversations have unveiled, reality paints a different picture, one where those whistling the tune aren't embracing ingenuity or heightened efficiency. Instead, they relinquish the battle altogether, succumbing to a sea of resignation and pompousness.

As we come to the end of this chapter, it's essential to explore the true impact of any pied piper's influence and compare it with the outcomes we had hoped for. What initially appeared as a simple mantra soon became more pervasive, affecting every aspect of our workplace dynamics and morale.

Initially, the appeal of "it is what it is" was its simplicity and ease of acceptance. However, its gradual spread overshadowed our once-vibrant atmosphere, fostering a culture of resignation and complacency. What started as a lighthearted phrase evolved into a mindset that blurred the lines between acceptance and indifference.

As we examine the current situation more closely, it's clear that the appeal of "it is what it is" still holds, but now it's causing significant problems. It's essential to recognize that this wasn't just an isolated incident but a symptom of broader issues within our organization. The failure of management to address these underlying problems allowed them to persist and worsen over time. Instead of promoting accountability and proactive problem-solving, there had been a shift toward evading responsibility and embracing a pessimistic outlook.

In a company culture situation such as this, the tendency to shift blame is evident not only among employees but also in management's actions. Rather than confronting issues directly, there's a tendency to resort to clichés like "it is what it is," perpetuating a cycle of mediocrity where mistakes go unchallenged and standards continue to decline.

What was concerning in my example above was that it was the first time we'd had to address such a cultural issue within our organization. I challenge you to consider how you would handle it if it crept into yours. What would you do? It highlights the need for introspection and corrective action before further harm is done. By shining a light on this influence and its negative consequences, a workplace can begin to move toward positive change.

Ultimately, this isn't about assigning blame but reclaiming our sense of purpose and pride in our work. We should look at ways to approach this disease that threatens to infect all workplaces everywhere. Remember, true success isn't measured by the absence of mistakes but by our willingness to learn from them and strive for improvement. It's time for us to examine the response to such attitudes and behaviors. It's time for us to jump into what we should do to get things back on track. *Now what?*

As we face the challenges ahead, it's crucial to remember that we have the power to shape our workplace culture. By promoting open communication, accountability, and shared responsibility, we can break free from complacent influence and create an environment where excellence flourishes.

In conclusion, the modern pied piper's influence reminds us of the importance of proactive leadership in preserving organizational culture. We can work toward a brighter future by acknowledging the gap between our intentions and outcomes.

How do you typically respond to change in your life? Are you someone who embraces change with enthusiasm, or do you tend to resist it?

Can you recall a recent change or transition in your life that challenged you? How did you navigate through it, and what did you learn from the experience?

Chapter Two

Know Yourself

Ultimately, the reason some of us do or don't eventually shrug the shoulders and say, "It is what it is," when workplace circumstances seem insurmountable or disheartening comes down to individual beliefs, characteristics, and personality styles. Let's dive into the fascinating world of personal dynamics. We all possess a unique blend of communication styles, leadership approaches, and personality types. The beauty lies in the diversity; there's no superior style or type. Like you, I've realized that being an individual means embracing many styles and traits. While you might lean toward one more than others, you're a mosaic of all sorts of factors.

Understanding who you are and how you communicate is paramount because who wants to be misunderstood? By delving into your style and how it interacts with others, you can easily navigate conflicts and misunderstandings, fostering effective communication. It's akin to watching your favorite TV show and seeing how each character brings their unique style into play. Just imagine one character with a passive-aggressive vibe, constantly pushing the buttons of the main character, leading to some epic revenge plots. Similarly, your leadership style is a compass, guiding you in motivating others and achieving your objectives. It's like having a direct route to success with your style paving the way forward.

Let's delve deeper into the diverse landscape of leadership styles and how they shape the dynamics of TV shows and the fabric of our workplaces. Consider the democratic leader, whose approach mirrors the inclusive nature of a well-written ensemble cast. Much like the characters in your favorite show, this leader values input from every team member, ensuring that decisions are made collectively, with everyone having an equal voice. It's akin to each character contributing their unique perspective to the storyline, enriching the narrative.

On the other hand, we have the coaching leader, embodying the nurturing essence of a mentor figure in a TV series. Just like a skilled showrunner recognizes and cultivates each character's strengths, this leader identifies and develops the talents of their team members. It's about fostering growth and empowerment, like guiding a character through their development arc on screen, helping to bring out the best—strengths—while incremental positive shifts in less strong areas emerge.

Now, let's tie this back to your personality type, the cornerstone of your interactions with others. Just as characters in a show have distinct traits that influence their actions and reactions, your behavioral tendencies shape how you engage with your colleagues. By understanding your unique blend of traits, you can adapt and refine your communication and leadership techniques, much like a seasoned actor bringing versatility to their performances.

Indeed, just as writers meticulously storyboard characters to ensure consistency and authenticity, understanding your communication style, leadership approach, and personality traits allows you to navigate fundamental life interactions with finesse. Whether you're leading a team meeting or collaborating on a project, this self-awareness empowers you to connect authentically with those around you, much like a well-scripted scene that resonates with viewers on a profound level.

I would encourage you to research different styles and personality types. I would love to tell you exactly which website to visit or which book to buy, but you will quickly see that many viewpoints vary from four styles to twenty-four different types. I just want you to understand that there are different styles and that you will lean toward several and other individuals will do the same. These styles influence how you interact with different people, which will affect your relationships, whether they are business or personal. The more you know about how you interact with others, the more you can choose responses instead of simply or habitually reacting.

Remember, one of the most essential components of any relationship is stopping and listening. We've all done it. I've done it. I know you've done it too; you're listening to someone talking, and you can't wait till they're done with their sentence so you can add your fascinating fact or your own story. What I realized was that I wasn't actually *listening* to the other person; instead, I was listening to my voice in my head. Don't get me wrong; there's nothing wrong with sharing your fact or story. Let the other person have their moment in the sun and finish what they say; then, when appropriate, add your two cents. They will appreciate that you're actively listening and caring about what they're saying. It will help a person to trust that you care and value them as an individual.

If you are a salesperson, paying attention to what the client says can help you close the deal. If it's a friend, give them the respect you want in a conversation. Relax and enjoy the discussion. With this world's fast-paced technology and instant messaging, we tend to glance at the screen and shoot back a response before we have read the whole message. We communicate in so many ways. Slow down and take the time to hear what is actually said and articulate a proper answer. After all, if you're not truly listening to what is being said, how can you effectively respond to the person you are talking to?

My journey to understand the different nuances of how I interacted with other employees came about when I became a manager. I noticed that several employees were not comprehending what I was saying. It was incredibly irritating. Sometimes I wonder to myself, "Am I even speaking English?"

I believed it was *their* problem at the time, but I quickly woke up and admitted to myself that it was me, not them. Then, I started looking into different management books and tools. I discovered that we all have different communication styles and leadership styles, and each of these interacts differently with the others.

Know Yourself

Let's delve deeper into the intricacies of communication styles and their impact on workplace dynamics, echoing the overarching theme of fostering employee satisfaction and engagement to ward off any pied piper's influence.

Picture this: You and one of the owners are direct communicators, much like characters in a well-scripted scene who cut straight to the chase. As you stride into the office, a quick exchange of hellos segues seamlessly into discussions about yesterday's accomplishments, today's tasks, and the division of responsibilities. It's like hitting the fast-forward button on productivity, a testament to your shared efficiency and mutual understanding of expectations.

However, not everyone thrives in this direct approach. Reflecting on my interactions with three distinct employees, it became evident that they craved a different rhythm. They needed a moment to share personal anecdotes about their day or beloved pets. Initially, as a stanch advocate for efficiency, I found it challenging to allocate precious time to these seemingly divergent conversations. In my mind, the manager's voice echoed, urging me to prioritize productivity over pleasantries.

Yet, something remarkable happened as I invested in these connections and listened attentively to their stories. The team's willingness to go the extra mile surged, illustrating the profound impact of feeling heard and valued. It was a strategic choice that nurtured camaraderie and served as a potent defense against disruptive influences.

While the direct approach may suit some, it's essential to recognize and accommodate diverse communication preferences. By embracing this diversity and fostering genuine connections, we fortify our workplaces against the pied piper's siren call, ensuring every team member feels seen, heard, and empowered to thrive.

There came a point when my morning routine started to shift, especially when dealing with those three specific colleagues. They had a different approach. They wanted me to ask how their day was shaping up and sometimes even share personal details. It was a bit of a switch for me. See, I'm more about getting things done, and for someone like me, stopping for five or ten minutes to listen and engage in a chat seemed like it could slow everything down. In my head, it was like the manager was yelling, *Time is money! Let's get to work.*

However, I soon realized that taking that extra time had its value. As I built stronger connections with these colleagues, something interesting happened. They seemed more willing to go the extra mile when I needed their support. And, here's the thing: I understood this wasn't just about hearing words; it was about being there, showing genuine interest, remembering, and understanding what they were saying. It was a bit of a balancing act because, sure, my work-focused side sometimes clashed with this approach.

But as time went on, I saw the results. The more I genuinely and actively listened, regardless of the time it took, the better our relationships became. It was like a secret strategy, keeping those negative or complacent vibes away. Looking back, it's clear that by showing my colleagues that they were seen and heard, I was keeping the team spirit alive and making our workplace happier. I was making a difference.

Back then, my leadership style leaned heavily toward being a pacesetter. As the production manager, the pressure was always to meet tight deadlines and ensure projects were delivered promptly. Our clients, often tied to event schedules, demanded precision timing, and any delay could jeopardize our long-term relationships.

In my pursuit of efficiency, I expected everyone to keep pace with my brisk tempo. However, this approach sometimes led to frustration when team members needed to match my speed. I couldn't understand why they weren't delivering as quickly or as consistently as I thought they should.

When I probed into the nuances of different leadership styles, I realized the flaw in my thinking. I had a "now-what? moment." I came to understand that not everyone operates at the same rhythm, and that's okay. Each team member possesses unique talents and strengths that I had overlooked in my quest for speed.

Learning to let go of the pressure to produce on my timeline, at my speed, and embracing the individuality of my team members was a turning point for me. I began to appreciate that the job could be completed just as effectively by 4:00 p.m. as it could by 2:00 p.m. By relinquishing my rigid expectations, I not only reduced my stress levels but also fostered a more positive and supportive work environment for everyone. In the end, the projects were still completed on time, and morale remained high, a testament to the power of adapting one's leadership style to fit the needs of the team.

I would immerse myself in different books such as this one to help me become a more rounded individual. Many years later, I joined Toastmasters. Those unfamiliar with the organization should know that it provides a supportive and positive place for members to develop communication, speaking, and leadership skills.

As we conclude our exploration of being willing to explore change, let's carry forward the wisdom gained from these pages. Let's embrace the challenges and opportunities that lie ahead, knowing that every now-what? moment holds the potential for transformation.

The journey from being mere managers to becoming effective leaders is not merely a transition in titles but a profound evolution in mindset and skillset. As we've examined the potential influence of the pied piper, it becomes abundantly clear why honing leadership skills is paramount.

Imagine yourself in a scenario where team morale is dwindling and productivity is on the decline. The pause and reflection on your relationship with your team members prompts you to ask, *Why should I look deeper, and what can I do?* This is your chance! This is your now-what? moment of truth. Here's where the importance of personal development, particularly in communication and leadership, shines through.

Consider a common workplace problem: Communication breakdowns lead to project delays and frustration among team members. By investing in personal training for leaders, you equip yourself with the tools to address these concerns head on. Through adept listening and understanding, you can unearth the root causes of these issues and implement effective solutions.

For instance, let's say you notice a pattern of miscommunication between different departments, causing bottlenecks in a project. By fostering unity and collaboration through improved communication channels and team-building exercises, you can mitigate these issues and cultivate a more harmonious work environment. When you effectively pause and examine the now-what? question, new ideas and a different way of thinking may emerge, but only if you are open to it.

By embracing these transformative steps, you're not just upgrading your leadership prowess, you're fostering a culture where team members feel valued, heard, and empowered. This shift from following the enchanting tune of complacency to the harmonious symphony of motivated teams is the hallmark of true leadership excellence.

Think about someone you admire for their resilience. Imagine how they may have been faced a challenge and stood up to it with their own now-what? moment. What qualities or characteristics do they possess that inspire you, and how can you incorporate these traits into your own life?

Reflect on the power of perspective in building resilience. How might reframing challenges or weaknesses as opportunities for growth enhance your ability to bounce back from adversity?

Chapter Three

Relativity of Responsibility

In the early part of the twentieth century, Albert Einstein published the theory of relativity. Don't worry. We're not going to have a physics lecture. But I would like you to think about classical relativity, which means there is no such thing as absolute motion or absolute rest. All objects, including you, move relative to each other. I would like you to think about this the next time you're riding in a car. Have a bottle of water with you. Let's say the vehicle is moving at thirty-five miles an hour down the street. You pick up your water bottle and pour the water into a cup. You perceive the water entering the cup as going zero miles an hour, when actually it's not. If your friend is standing on the sidewalk as you drive by, your friend will see the water traveling at thirty-five miles an hour. At this point, you're probably wondering what I'm trying to get at.

Let's take a look at Michael and Camila. Michael is a graffiti artist working by the riverfront, painting a mural on the levy. Camila works across the street as a financial adviser. She can see Michael from her office window and observes Michael, the artist, working throughout the day from her own desk.

Michael uses a piece of chalk and roughly sketches out his idea on the wall. He then grabs his boxes of spray paints. As Michael moves up and down the ladder, carefully spraying each color on the levy wall, the mural starts to take shape, and what once was a plain wall becomes a work of art. The time it took to make the mural was long and arduous for Michael, but to Camila, it went quickly and easily. Classic relativity states that motion is relative to the observer's activity state. Camila was sitting back and watching, and Michael was in the throes of doing. Keep this in mind when you think someone isn't working at the pace you think they should be or when you think something went quickly and smoothly. Camila was not aware of the weeks of planning or Michael's stress of the day. Things look different from various vantage points.

People don't always recognize how much thought and effort others may have put into something in their own planning stages. It is wise to listen to others, look beyond what you think you see, and always be willing to ask questions. I think we are all familiar with the images of the three little monkeys, one covering his eyes, the second covering his ears, and the third covering his mouth. There is some debate on the origin of these three monkeys and their meanings. But let's consider the three wise monkeys at the Toshogu shrine in Nikko, Japan.

It Is What It Is

These three wise little monkeys date back to the sixteenth century. They were initially part of a Japanese proverb: Mizaru sees no evil and covers his eyes, Kikazaru hears no evil and covers his years, and Iwazaru speaks no evil, covering his mouth. These three little guys were initially seen as wise, keeping from these evils. Later, they were portrayed as having a lack of moral responsibility to show how people refuse to know their wrongdoings and essentially look the other way and not take responsibility for their own actions. Can you see each of the little monkeys saying, "It is what it is," as they cover their respective parts? This concept has endured for centuries, illustrating how these monkeys symbolize more than just shirking responsibility. They also embody the virtues of taking pride in one's work and facing life's challenges head-on.

The pied piper would like us to make excuses and not take responsibility for our actions. He would love us to throw up our hands, shrug our shoulders, and say, "It is what it is." Instead of flipping this and asking, "Now what?," we try to justify, blame, or excuse ourselves to keep from being accountable. I saw this many times at work when a job would go south. An employee would look me straight in the face and make excuses to keep the blame off them.

Consequently, I blamed myself for something going wrong when the failures were not just one thing or one person. One person was not stepping up and taking responsibility, and the other one would bear the full brunt of things to a fault, making them the martyr. Neither one wins. One never grows as a person, and the other becomes angry or even depressed because they *think* it's not good enough no matter what they do. One needs to take responsibility for their actions, and the other needs to take a step back, know the truth of the situation, and make the proper adjustments to keep moving forward. The person playing the martyr is the one who should stop and call out the others to take accountability for their actions. For those who like to point fingers at everyone else but themselves, think of the saying that when you point the finger at someone, three fingers are pointing back at you.

What's the difference between an excuse and a reason? According to the Oxford Dictionary, a reason is a cause, explanation, or justification for an action or an event. In contrast, the definition of an excuse is to attempt to lessen the blame.

Let's look at Sharon and Patty's interaction when Patty was an hour and a half late for work. Sharon was a manager at a restaurant, and Patty was supposed to arrive at work at 6:00 a.m. to work the breakfast shift, but she did not arrive until 7:30 a.m. Patty apologized to Sharon, explaining that she didn't get to sleep until 1:00 a.m. because she got caught up in watching a late-night movie and forgot to set her alarm clock. Sharon could only think of these as excuses, but to Patty, they were all part of her argument, her reasons for why she could not make it to work on time.

The reality is that Patty did not take responsibility for getting to work on time. Her reasons were really just excuses. Neither Sharon nor the rest of the morning shift appreciated Patty not being there on time. It put more of a workload on the rest of the team to get the breakfast shift started. Patty seemed oblivious that the manager and the rest of the team were upset with her. She had given her so-called reasons to them, but she was not taking responsibility for her actions, which caused the others around her to have different feelings and emotions.

It seemed like a storm was brewing within the team with Patty in the eye. Her repeated tardiness and lack of accountability left a bitter taste in the mouths of many, including the manager. Fellow employees saw a lack of any consequences for her behaviors and began contemplating adopting similar habits. At the same time, the manager hesitated to take drastic measures like termination, but Patty's pattern of behavior was hard to ignore.

The issue wasn't just Patty's habitual lateness, it was also her apparent disregard for the impact of her actions on the team dynamics. Despite the mounting frustration from her colleagues, Patty carried on as if nothing had happened, exacerbating tensions within the group. Some viewed her demeanor as insincere and arrogant, while others questioned the point of punctuality if Patty didn't see fit to adhere to it.

In the midst of it all, the tune of the pied piper emerged, settled in, and then seemed to resonate louder than ever, luring others into a sense of resignation with its refrain. Patty's failure to acknowledge her role in the disruption only fueled and perpetuated a cycle of indifference and discord.

Yet, Patty's reluctance to take ownership of her actions wasn't just detrimental to her reputation at the restaurant; it also seeped into her relationships outside of work as well. While many genuinely liked Patty, her unreliability and inclination for excuses tarnished her in the eyes of others. It was as if she was stuck in a loop, singing the same tune of excuses while those around her grew weary. Her failure to acknowledge that she was the common denominator of the collapse of workplace and interpersonal relationships began to isolate her.

Ultimately, the truth has a way of surfacing, even amid a chorus of excuses. Patty's unwillingness to confront the reality of her actions only prolonged the discord, highlighting the importance of honesty and accountability in fostering healthy relationships, both in the workplace and beyond. This would have been the perfect opportunity for Patty to pause, take responsibility, and then ask herself *Now what?*

Amid these challenges, it's crucial to recognize the role of leadership in fostering accountability and empowering team members. Just as Patty's story illustrates the consequences of failing to take ownership of one's actions, there's another pitfall that managers must avoid: the temptation to do a coworker's job.

Relativity of Responsibility

I've emphasized the importance of thinking outside the box and utilizing critical thinking to solve problems. It's about going that extra mile to ensure the job gets done. But as a manager, it's equally important to resist the urge to step in and take over tasks that belong to team members.

Consider Connie, a manager at a small auto care shop, who faced an issue with one of her mechanics neglecting to replenish windshield wiper fluid as part of a standard oil change. Instead of empowering the mechanic to take responsibility for his duties, Connie assumed the blame and failed to communicate the full scope of the service to him.

Just like a parent teaching a child to ride a bike, you start with training wheels, offering support and encouragement. But eventually, you must let go and allow them to ride on their own. Similarly, as a manager, it's essential to empower your team to take responsibility for their actions and decisions.

So, the question for you is this: How can you empower your team members to take ownership of their responsibilities while still providing support and guidance?

By guiding and supporting your team members without doing everything for them, you foster growth, independence, and a culture of accountability within your organization. Remember, effective leadership isn't about doing the work for your team; it's about equipping them with the tools and resources they need to succeed on their own. Workplace issues have many roots besides leadership and communication styles. Navigating generational differences in the workplace can also be like deciphering a complex puzzle. Each generation brings its own set of values, way of conveying information, and work preferences, style, and ethics to the table, which can sometimes clash with those of other generations. For instance, older generations might view younger colleagues as entitled or lacking in work ethic. In comparison, younger generations may see their older counterparts as resistant to change or out of touch with modern trends.

To bridge these gaps and unite employees or teams, it is imperative to foster a culture of understanding, respect, and collaboration. This starts with acknowledging and valuing the unique perspectives and contributions of each generation. Encouraging open dialogue and creating opportunities for intergenerational mentorship can help break down barriers and facilitate knowledge sharing. Additionally, implementing flexible work arrangements and embracing technology can accommodate diverse work styles and preferences, allowing employees of all generations to thrive.

Those in charge can also usher change and lead by example by demonstrating inclusivity and actively seeking input from employees across generations when making decisions or implementing new systems. By celebrating diversity and leveraging the strengths of each generation, people can harness the power of generational differences to drive innovation, creativity, and success. Ultimately, by fostering a culture of unity and collaboration, teams can overcome the it-is-what-it-is mindset and work together toward common goals.

In concluding this chapter, we've sorted through the intricate dynamics of responsibility, viewing it with the lens of relativity and the timeless wisdom of the three monkeys. Just as motion is relative to the observer's perspective, so too is the perception of effort, dedication, and accountability in the workplace. We've seen how Michael's artistic endeavor appeared differently to Camila, highlighting the importance of understanding varying viewpoints.

Moreover, we've confronted the pied piper's seductive call to absolve ourselves of responsibility with the casual mantra. Through Patty's story, we've discerned the fine line between reasons and excuses, realizing that ownership of actions is pivotal for growth and trust. Patty's reluctance to take responsibility affected her relationships and hindered her progress in the workplace.

Yet, amid these challenges, we've also explored the issue of generational differences and their impact on workplace dynamics. By fostering a culture of understanding, respect, and collaboration, organizations can harness the unique perspectives of each generation to drive innovation and success. By embracing inclusivity, encouraging open dialogue, and leveraging the strengths of each generation, teams can overcome the it-is-what-it-is mindset and unite toward common goals.

So let us echo the timeless wisdom that when we point a finger at others, we acknowledge how we are also to blame. With each honest step forward, we can learn to dismantle the siren's song and foster a culture of authenticity and accountability, where it's not just "it is what it is," but what we actively shape and refine through the question of "Now what?"

Are you aware of any patterns in your behavior that could be seen as expressing frustration indirectly?

Think about a situation in which fear held you back from pursuing a goal or opportunity. What steps can you take to confront and overcome that fear, allowing courage to guide your actions?

Imagine yourself taking courageous action toward a long-held dream or aspiration. What small, incremental steps can you take today to move closer to that vision?

Chapter Four

The Summer of 1969

It Is What It Is

Looking back, it seems to me that the pied piper was fast asleep in 1969. It was an awe-inspiring time. Humans stepped foot on the moon's surface for the first time. Astronaut Neil Armstrong said his famous words, "That's one small step for man, one giant leap for mankind." The entire world was captivated by new possibilities.

As the sultry summer of 1969 enveloped the Midwest, my mother, burdened by the oppressive heat and her pregnancy, often lamented the discomfort. Lockjaw plagued her, limiting her dietary options to orange popsicles. Then, one early Tuesday morning, the moment arrived, and I was poised to enter the world. My father, awakened by my mother, joined her in anticipation of my grandmother's arrival to care for my older brother, Johnny. Unlike Johnny, who had taken his time to arrive, I wasted no time, prompting a swift journey to the hospital. Within an hour or so, I made my debut, ushered into a world where Bugs Bunny's antics awaited me on the television screen.

Transitioning into the 1970s, I found myself as a latchkey kid, a term that epitomized the independence afforded to children of that era. Home alone, I abided by a set of simple rules set by my mother:

The Summer of 1969

Enter the house and stay put.

Enjoy a snack of chips and soda, and most importantly, when your brother arrives, obey his authority, an unspoken decree that shaped our sibling dynamic.

Lucky for me, I had an awesome big brother. He never minded my tagging along, and he was always up for entertaining me. One of my fondest memories is of him reading to me from a book that contained snippets of all sorts of information. One chapter revealed why things were the way they were and what made them tick. One chapter was about animals and explained why skunks smell so bad. Another chapter explained why the sky is blue. We spent hours with this book and others that would make me question many things. Yes, I was definitely the kind of kid who always asked why. I was so curious that sometimes I would even occasionally disassemble a toy just to see how it worked.

When the weekend came, my father would call my brother and me to him. It would be project time. Usually, this meant he had a project that my brother and I would be tasked with, and my father would oversee our work. In retrospect, it may have been just tasks to keep us occupied for hours on end.

He once wanted my brother to move a large crate of heavy electrical equipment from one end of the shop to the other. He told my brother to take the heavy pieces out, drag the crate across the room and into the corner and put all the components back into the box. With that set of instructions, my father turned and went back into the house.

I was too little to be any real help to my brother, so I stood there looking up at him, watching him stare at the crate, hands on his hips, looking at the box, then looking into the corner and looking back at the large wooden mission as if awaiting divine providence. Then I noticed him looking around the room. He started nodding his head up and down in agreement with his hidden ideas. A slight grin danced in the corners of his mouth. This was the first time I noticed the wheels turning in someone's mind. Finally, he looked over at me and said, "Come with me."

We went over to an old oil drum where we had all sorts of broom handles and dowel rods stored, and he pulled one of the dowel rods out and commanded me to gather up all the dowel rods that were that diameter and take them over to the crate. He then marched over, snatched a four-foot prybar off the wall, and scooped up two chunks of wood that we used to wedge the doors open. As he hurried back toward the crate, I noticed he was deep in thought.

"Okay," he said. "I want you to be careful, but when I lift the corner of the crate, I need you to wedge in this chunk of wood and stand back."

We duplicated this task on both sides of the crate, lifting it about an inch and a half on one end. He then slid several of the dowel rods underneath the box, then pulled out the wedges. We did the same thing to the other side of the crate, where he put a couple more dowel rods underneath the container.

He looked sternly at me and said, "Stand back. I don't want you getting hurt."

Then he went to the back of the crate. He put both hands on the back of the box, tilted his head down, looked at the floor, lunged his feet backward, and started to push the crate. It began to roll; his head popped up from behind the crate. He was grinning from ear to ear. He picked up three of the dowel rods from the rear of the container.

He began wagging them at me saying, "That's how you do it."

He repeated the process of moving the dowel rods under the crate and rolling them until they were all the way across the room into the appointed corner without removing one single piece of equipment from the crate.

That day, I learned that if you stop and think about a task, there may be more than one way to achieve your desired outcome.

Many years later, I was tasked with accompanying our sales rep, Kimberly, for an installation. The owners wanted me there in case the installers we hired needed help. We were heading up north, about a six-hour drive, where we would meet the employed installers the next morning. We were bringing them thirteen large panels of cut vinyl that they would apply to the wall, along with fifteen plexiglass photos of all the clients' properties. The first day, the installers and I applied all the cut vinyl to the wall. There were only a few tiny hiccups, but nothing that a little patience couldn't fix. The following day, the installers would drill into the walls for the standoffs that would hold the plexiglass pictures in position.

Everything was going smoothly; the installers were finishing up the last pieces of plexiglass, and I cleaned up all the trash. Kimberly was pleased because we were on time for the walk-through. She gave everything a final look, and that's when she saw it. A big scratch on one of the pieces of plexiglass. She turned to the installers and pointed it out.

They walked over, looked at the scratch, and told her, "Yep, that's a scratch."

She asked them whether they could fix it, at which point they just stared at her. Kimberly did not hear the pied piper, but I heard him loud and clear. Finally, she looked over at me, and I asked them if they had brought a rubbing compound that could buff out the scratch; they replied no, they did not have any. Kimberly asked if I had brought some. To my chagrin, I also had none. Even though in my youth, I was a proud member of Boy Scout Explorer Troop 514 with the motto of always being prepared, that's the one thing I forgot to pack.

Kimberly was starting to pace; looking at her phone, she turned and told me that the clients would be there in twenty minutes to do the walk-through.

"What are we going to do?" she anxiously asked.

First, I found myself standing at the wall gazing at all the work that had been done. Then, with both hands on my hips, not saying a word but thinking *Now what?* I let the wheels in my mind start turning. Finally, I felt a slight grin emerge to match my thoughts, and I told Kimberly I'd be back shortly.

She asked, "Where are you going?"

I replied, "I'm going to run up to the hotel room. I'll be back in a minute."

As I walked across the property to the hotel side, I could hear her exclaiming and shaking her phone at me, "They're all going to be here in twenty minutes!"

When I got to the hotel room, I hurriedly picked up two washcloths. I ran one of the washcloths under the faucet, ringing most of the water out and making it damp. Then I collected my toothpaste off the counter and proceeded back down to where Kimberly was nervously awaiting. As I approached her, it was clear she was frazzled. Finally, she asked if I would be able to fix the scratch.

I looked at her with a smile from ear to ear and exclaimed, "Just watch!"

The Summer of 1969

I used my toothpaste as a buffing compound and proceeded to buff out the scratch on the piece of plexiglass. I removed the excess toothpaste with the wet cloth and finished wiping the plexiglass to a beautiful shine with the dry one.

I turned and said, "The scratch is gone, and it is also minty fresh."

At this point, Kimberly smiled as she always had, and she shook her head and rolled her eyes at me. As I turned to put the toothpaste and wash-cloths into my installer's bag, the general manager, the head of maintenance, and the director of marketing, along with two other marketing people, came for the walk-through. I gave Kimberly a little wink, and she proceeded to gush over how beautiful their wall looked. There is nothing better in business than a happy customer and a happy sales rep.

That darn pied piper had his way with those three installers but not me. I wasn't going to disappoint the sales rep or disappoint a client. I found another way to solve the mess, and all it took was a tube of toothpaste and a little patience. By no means do I think I'm smarter than anyone else, but I do know that I have the desire to strive for something better. Can you imagine what our lives would be like if most people just tried a little harder or aimed for a higher objective?

Reflect on the lessons from these stories and consider how you can apply them in your life and leadership journey. Encourage curiosity, critical thinking, and innovation not only within yourself but also in those around you. Create an environment where asking, "Now what?" and exploring different perspectives are welcomed and encouraged.

In the fast-paced world we live in, it's easy to fall into the trap of complacency. The enchanting tune often lures us into a state of contentment with the status quo. But let's not forget that actual progress and growth stem from a willingness to challenge the norm, to question that mindset, and to seek out unconventional solutions to age-old problems.

The other day, I was scrolling on my phone watching various videos, when one caught my eye and made me laugh. It featured a silly golden retriever proudly carrying a stick that was almost twice her size. As she ran with the stick, her tail wagging in excitement, she attempted to take it down a path to her owner. However, the path was surrounded by trees, and the stick kept getting caught on them.

The poor golden retriever pushed through some saplings, but then the stick inevitably got caught on a larger tree, causing her fun-loving demeanor to turn into frantic frustration. Despite the obstacles, you could hear the owner laughing and cheering the dog on. Eventually, the retriever began to realize that it needed to reframe its approach to getting the stick to its owner.

After several frustrating attempts, the dog finally dropped the stick. The owner reassured the dog that it was okay, but then something remarkable happened. The dog suddenly spun around, grabbed the stick on one end, and began running backward with excitement toward the owner. It was clear that the golden retriever had reframed her mindset and found a new way to accomplish her goal.

What I learned from this delightful video is that even though the golden retriever initially felt overwhelmed by the seemingly simple task of delivering the stick to its owner, she eventually realized the importance of assessing the situation and breaking it down into more manageable components. In her case, simply dropping the stick and grasping it at one end allowed her to move it down the path. The retriever's instinct to brainstorm different solutions to her problem exemplifies a valuable lesson: Setting realistic goals and strategizing potential solutions can lead to success. Similarly, in our own lives, tackling tasks by priority and identifying specific challenges through brainstorming can pave the way for effective problem-solving. Whether it's delegating tasks or seeking support from colleagues and friends, adopting a proactive approach can help us overcome the obstacles we face.

When faced with challenges, remember to pause and consider alternative solutions. Encourage brainstorming sessions with others where no idea is too wild or unconventional. Foster a culture where mistakes are seen as opportunities for growth and learning rather than failures to be feared.

Aspire to be a leader who does so by example, demonstrating resourcefulness and resilience in the face of adversity. Empower your team members to take ownership of problems and explore creative solutions independently. Provide support and guidance when needed, but also trust in their abilities to think critically and find innovative solutions.

The journey from complacency to creativity begins with a single step. One that requires us to challenge the notion of good enough and instead embrace the belief that anything is possible with the right mindset and approach.

Above all, strive to cultivate a mindset of continuous improvement and excellence. Encourage a relentless pursuit of better ways of doing things, never settling for mediocrity. Challenge yourself and those around you to constantly push the boundaries of what is possible, finding the now-what? moments.

This chapter illuminates the transformative potential of defying the pied piper's seductive melody and embracing the ethos of creative problem-solving. It underscores the importance of fostering a culture where curiosity, critical thinking, and innovation are encouraged and celebrated. By challenging the notion of it is what it is and embracing the now-what? moments, we open ourselves to a world of endless possibilities.

As leaders, it is incumbent upon us to cultivate an environment where creativity flourishes and where team members feel encouraged and empowered to explore unconventional solutions and embrace the unknown. This fosters open communication, and we can inspire our teams to push the boundaries of what is possible as we strive for excellence in all endeavors.

In the symphony of possibility, let us harmonize our efforts, drawing strength from our inner creative spark to forge a path toward progress. Together, let us defy the pied piper's allure and create our unique melody of success, making a meaningful difference not only in our work but also in the world around us.

Reflect on a recent change or transition in your life. How did you initially respond to the change, and what emotions did you experience during the process?

Think about a recent situation where you encountered difficulty in achieving a goal. Did you consider alternative approaches or strategies, or did you feel stuck in one mindset?

Imagine yourself as a navigator, confidently steering through the waters of change toward new horizons. What mindset shifts or tools can you cultivate to embrace change as an opportunity for growth and renewal?

Chapter Five

The Dawn of Mankind

It Is What It Is

What would our lives be like if the good-enough attitude been present at the dawn of mankind? Would you even be here? You could guess that anyone under the spell wouldn't last very long, given that the pied piper's little adage encourages letting things go and quitting when the going gets tough or when there's any kind of unpleasantness. However, at the beginning of time, individuals were problem-solvers and go-getters. For obvious reasons, only the strongest and most intelligent survived. You didn't have to outrun the tiger. You just had to outrun the person next to you.

There are so many things throughout our history that you could reference when it comes to the now-what? attitude: making fire, the wheel, discovering bronze, the combustible engines, and the list goes on and on. If people don't stop and consider new and different ways to take the initiative, we don't push forward. Technology, the arts, and humanity would certainly suffer if we succumb to it-is-what-it-is mentality. Let's look at three individuals in our recent history who made life easier and safer because they stopped and concluded there was a need to push forward with a solution. Women at the turn of the twentieth century scarcely had any opportunities other than to become homemakers, domestic workers, nurses, or maybe typists, with even fewer for women of color. This is why I would like to introduce you to Alice Parker. She was born in 1895 and grew up in New Jersey. She attended a high school academy connected to Howard University and, in 1910, earned a certificate with honors from the academy. On December 23, 1919, Alice was granted patent #1,325,905 for a gas-fired furnace with a heat exchanger distributing warm air through air ducts.

Until this time, there were two common ways to heat your home: through burning coal or wood. Coal was primarily used in cast iron stoves or used to heat boilers to distribute steam through pipes. Of course, we now know coal is not the cleanest of burning fuels, and boilers and steam pipes sometimes exploded if overheated. The other common source of heat was wood. Today, many of us still enjoy the smell of a crackling fire in the fireplace, but imagine that being the only heat source in a home, and how a fireplace or stove in every room would have been needed to thoroughly heat the home. How would you like to chop wood every day so that you could stay warm? During this period, many homes and businesses burned to the ground when cinders from the fireplace ignited the primarily wooden houses throughout the United States.

Alice saw a need not only to keep the majority of the heat from escaping through the chimney but also the need for a safer alternative. She tinkered and tried many iterations before coming up with her version of a heat exchanger. Unfortunately, her patent was never produced, but it was the forerunner of early natural gas heating systems. We should consider thanking Alice Parker for our safe, warm homes.

The next gentleman I would like you to know is Lewis Latimer, the son of escaped enslaved people. Lewis was born in 1848 in Massachusetts and became one of the first great African American inventors, working alongside the likes of Thomas Edison and Alexander Graham Bell. Despite the challenges he faced, including racial prejudice and societal barriers, Latimer refused to succumb to the pied piper's discouraging tune. In a world where obstacles seemed insurmountable and opportunities scarce, Latimer found his now-what? moment among the drafting tables of a patent law firm. His decision to teach himself mechanical drawing and pursue a career as a draftsman marked the beginning of his remarkable journey as an inventor and innovator. Through sheer determination and perseverance, Latimer defied the odds and made invaluable contributions to the field of electrical engineering.

Hiram Maxum was Thomas Edison's rival and one of the founders of the US Electric Lighting Company. In 1879, Latimer found himself working as an assistant manager and draftsman. Here, he invented a modification for making carbon filaments for a more substantial and longer-lasting carbonization process, which meant a lightbulb with a longer life. Latimer worked in New York with Thomas Edison, where he wrote the first book on electric lighting entitled *Incandescent Electric Lighting*. He also worked as a supervisor installing public electric lights throughout New York and Philadelphia. He was a founding member of Edison Pioneers, where he was the only person of color. Lewis Latimer helped many inventors receive their patents because of his drafting ability. He is also credited with his patents for improvements to existing inventions. When you flip the light switch on or walk around your town at night, feeling safe and secure, think of Lewis Latimer.

This next story starts on a tragic note. George Blodgett was the director of General Electric's patent department. Late one night in 1897 in Sche-nectady, New York, he interrupted a home invasion where he was fatally shot, leaving his young son and pregnant wife. Several weeks later, Katharine Burr Blodgett was born. The shattered family moved to New York City, hoping that the bustling town would have more opportunities for a widow. Several years later, the family moved to France and then Germany. Mrs. Blodgett hoped that her young children would be immersed in other cultures at a young age. Finally, they returned to New York City, where Blodgett continued her education at Rayson School. She then received her bachelor's degree at Bryn Mawr College. Despite the tragic circumstances that surrounded her early life, Blodgett refused to be defined by despair and resignation. Instead, she found her now-what? moment in the halls of the General Electric laboratory.

When Blodgett was eighteen, she visited the General Electric laboratory where her father had worked. She met Irving Langmuir, a physicist who knew her father. He proceeded to give her a tour of the facility, where he recognized her passion and understanding of physics. He explained that if she received a master's degree in physics, she could work in this field one day. She took Langmuir's words to heart and went to the University of Chicago, earning her degree. Irving Langmuir was a man of his word, so she began to work at the General Electric Company, where she was the very first woman research scientist. Blodgett worked alongside Langmuir for many years. He encouraged her to advance her career by getting a PhD. He managed to use his professional clout to help get her into Cambridge University, where she was the first woman to receive a PhD in physics. She then returned to the General Electric laboratories and continued to work with Irving. Their work on films only a few molecules thick was groundbreaking. The Langmuir-Blodgett film is transferred from liquid gas to a solid surface. The forerunners for nonreflective coatings include eyeglasses, camera lenses, microscopes, displays, electronic circuits, and even periscopes for submarines. In addition, Katharine developed a color gauge to measure the thickness of thin films, which soon became the standard. She later worked on several wartime technologies, including a better smokescreen, which lingered in the air for a more extended time, helping to save many lives during the invasion of France and Italy during World War II. She also helped to improve better methods of deicing airplanes. So, the next time you travel safely via plane in winter or binge watch a program, you have Katharine Blodgett to thank for the clarity of the camera lens and much more.

The three individuals you just read about are a minute part of our history. The pioneers of our past ignited a torch for us to see our way forward in hopes that each generation will also light the way for the next, ensuring we flourish. I encourage you to devour as many biographies as possible, and by doing this, you will learn how other individuals overcame, triumphed, understood, and even failed—often many times—before they succeeded.

Now, as we draw this chapter to a close, let's consider how the stories of triumph and persever-ance we've encountered can inspire us to overcome our own challenges.

From the annals of history emerge stories of in-dividuals who, like modern-day pied piper defiers, rose to the occasion with determination and inge-nuity. The likes of Alice Parker, Lewis Latimer, and Katharine Burr Blodgett remind us that the journey to progress is paved with the stones of persistence. They navigated uncharted territories, shattered limitations, and overcame adversities, lighting the path for generations to come.

Alice Parker's pioneering vision for a safer and more efficient way to heat our homes speaks to the power of disruptive thinking. Lewis Latimer's unsung contributions to essential inventions reveal the significance of a steadfast draftsman and a forward-thinking mind. Katharine Burr Blodgett's relentless pursuit of innovation, even in the face of personal tragedy, showcases the strength that resides within a determined heart.

This chapter is a call to leaders and managers, a reminder that in times of controversy and adversity, the siren call of the pied piper can seem alluring. It's easy to lose sight of the broader picture when the tempest rages. But through the stories of those who paved the way before us, we learn that even in the darkest hours, embracing tenacity and shunning surrender can forge a path toward remarkable solutions.

As we navigate the complexities of modern workplaces, where challenges are constant companions, let us remember the dawn of mankind. Let us remember the courage that propelled our ancestors to conquer the unknown and let us infuse our leadership with that same spirit. When the melodies of doubt and resignation beckon, may we stand strong, undeterred by the piper's call. Instead, may we rally our teams, inspire innovation, and forge ahead with unwavering determination.

Just as our forebearers refused to yield, so too can we rise above the discord and uncertainty that may cloud our path. Let's recognize the allure for what it is: an illusion that promises an easy way out. In its place, let's embrace the ethos of those who came before us, pioneers who, through sheer tenacity, illuminated the path forward with their own now-what? moment. With each step we take, we defy the nonchalance, lighting the torch of progress for our teams, our businesses, and generations yet to come.

Imagine yourself a year from now, having fully embraced change and pursued your goals with passion and determination. What steps can you take today to make this vision a reality? What support or resources might you need along the way?

See yourself embodying a mindset of abundance and gratitude in every aspect of your life. What small, intentional actions can you take each day to cultivate a deeper sense of gratitude and appreciation?

Chapter Six

Defying the Pied Piper's Call

It Is What It Is

The fourteenth century English proverb says, "The great oak was once a little nut that held its ground."

The mentality of the it-is-what-it-is movement does not wish for us to take root, grow, and blossom into all the glorious possibilities that lie before us. But this simple proverb reminds us that great and mighty things can come from the simplest and smallest things.

I would like you to meet Pamela. In 1984, she was diagnosed with a grade 3 brain tumor. Pamela and her husband, Tom, were blindsided by the doctor's diagnosis. Pamela had put off going to the doctor because she thought the headaches and memory loss were just from the stress of managing a family: They had eighteen-month-old baby boy, Jacob, and their daughter, Jenny, who was just starting kindergarten. Pamela convinced herself that the persistent nausea just meant she needed to take better care of herself. She made it a priority and got a little more sleep and started eating better, but then she had her first seizure, which changed everything.

The doctor told Pamela and Tom the inescapable fact that she had less than a year to live. The doctor proceeded to tell them how he would manage the tumor. Pamela sat there nodding her head with agreement, holding Tom's hand tightly but not hearing what was said. All she could think of was Jacob and Jenny and how they would have to grow up without a mother, and how Tom's life would change forever, becoming a single father.

As they were driving home, they vowed that she would beat cancer and that no matter what, Tom and Pamela loved each other and would cherish the time they had left. Then, a calm came over Pamela, and she turned to Tom and said, "Let's go shopping." At first, Tom was amused by her comment, thinking it was a joke, but Pamela was serious. "Tom, we need a video camera and tape recorder, and I need greeting cards, as well as stationery," Pamela exclaimed.

In the last months of her life, Pamela and Tom made videos and tape recordings for the children. They did simple things like recording bedtime stories so the children could still hear her voice to lull them to sleep. As she made the tape recordings, her dreams were that someday they could play them to her grandchildren and that they'd know Grandma in a small way.

It Is What It Is

Tom set up the video camera, and Pamela sat on the couch talking for hours about both children's births. She talked about the things she remembered like how when Jenny was born, her little nose was all smooshed on her face, and that's why she has such a cute little turned up nose. And when Jacob was born, he had so much hair that they almost called him Sampson. She gave them both advice on the videotape that only a mother can offer. On one of the videotapes for Jenny, Pamela held up a lady's blue, lace handkerchief and told the story of how it was her great-grandmother's and that it had been passed down at the wedding of her grandmother, her mother, and to her on her wedding day. "Every bride needs something blue," she told Jenny. Tom was instructed to hand a beautifully wrapped wedding gift to Jenny when it was time to watch the video.

She bought two stationery sets at the store, one for Jacob and one for Jenny. She wrote heartfelt letters to both of them that she instructed Tom to give them at certain milestones in their lives. Some of the letters to the children were simple little pick-me-up notes for when they felt blue or a little lost. She wanted to ensure that her children always knew that she was close by and holding their hands even if she couldn't physically be there.

She made nine audiotapes, five videotapes, and 103 cards and letters for her children. Pamela fought a valiant battle for eight months. Tom remarried six years later. As a result, Jacob and Jenny gained two stepbrothers who were also in awe of their mother, Pamela.

You see, the pied piper would like you to think that something as inescapable as death should cause you to throw your hands up and say, "It is what it is." But Pamela did not hear the chant; instead, she listened to her own magical tune that she would teach her children to sing to their children. Tom could've been bitter and angry, but he chose to honor Pamela's memory so that when he moved on with his life, he knew she would not be forgotten.

We have all said, "I just knew that would happen at one time or another." So here is a story about a project on which we tried our hardest to avoid as many hurdles as possible, knowing full well that on such a large project, we were sure to stumble, but at the end of the day, we had to persevere and finish the job.

This story is another illustration that underscores the importance of refusing to yield to surrender. It involves the narrative of a remarkable team, embodying a proactive approach in the face of project challenges.

It was 2:00 p.m., and Kimberly had just returned from her big meeting with the museum. She grabbed the two owners and told me to gather the computer and production teams and meet her in the conference room. Everybody was thrilled that we had gotten the year's biggest show. Kimberly was very animated as she started pulling out the paperwork, showing us all the printing that we would be producing, ranging from detailed descriptions to specifics: plaques, wallpaper, and a monumental sign that would hang from the ceiling at the entranceway for everyone to see.

I always enjoyed the museum shows. It guaranteed that the whole office would be bustling for at least a month. With an entire show added to our regular workload, I was highly motivated with no room for just "good enough." I admit, this is where I buddied up to Mr. Murphy instead. I think most of you have heard of Mr. Murphy and his Law. If you haven't, let me take a moment and introduce you to him. Murphy's Law basically states that anything that *can* go wrong, will.

Part of my job as a manager was to figure out what could go wrong before it did and avoid it if possible. This is why I sat down with Mr. Murphy and tried to figure out how he planned to trip up the project. As we went through each section of the show, everyone on the team expressed their concerns and developed possible solutions before moving forward. But no matter how well anyone plans, Mr. Murphy just might get through.

In this particular case, it was on our grand entranceway sign. (And man, was it grand!) The specifications for the sign were to be 98 x 119 x 1, one piece, lightweight, and white so that we could print on it but with a black border. Kimberly asked me if we had a substrate that would work. I smiled at her and said, "Sure, I'll get a sheet of kryptonite brought in overnight." She never did like my Superman joke, but it always made me smile when she had already sold something to a client that didn't necessarily exist (yet).

It Is What It Is

Kimberly and I started looking at our options and settled on seaming two sheets of one-inch clad foam board together. Kimberly had talked to the museum, and they were okay with a small seam keeping the panels together.

As it was printing, one of the technicians asked, "Is that going to fit through the doors?" I told him I wasn't sure, and to follow me as I grabbed the tape measure. We ran the tape measure across the door opening, and it came to ninety-four inches.

He looked at me bewildered and said, "Now what are we going to do?"

As he was still holding the tape measure against the doorframe, I smiled and said we would just carry it at an angle, and I raised my arm higher, increasing the angle and giving us more space to move the sign into the cutting room.

As I finished the graphic at the end of the day, using a single stripe of one-inch black gaffer's tape around the edge, Kimberly came in to inspect it. She asked if we could package it up for tomorrow's delivery. I assured her that we could and hoped it would fit in the truck.

As Kimberly's eyes popped, she realized she had not thought of that. I could only keep a straight face for a couple of seconds, and I started to smile and laugh and said, "Don't worry, it'll fit in a box truck."

Many hurdles can be avoided, and even when one pops up, you should be able to find an alternative solution if you look hard enough. Stop and take the time to look. Don't be afraid to ask other people for their opinions. You obviously do not know everything. Like everyone in the conference room, we all expressed our concerns and came up with solutions before the project started. When we come upon obstacles, we figure a way to go around, over, or through them, and so can you.

Not trying, standing by, and being negligent is how any pied piper likes to work. He looks for individuals who lack ambition or who have no determination or weak goals in life. I know this seems harsh, but I have witnessed that as soon as the pied piper can make an unmotivated person say, "It is what it is," the chorus of everyone else may quickly follow. There are many reasons why others join in. Some see how easy it is to sing the sweet melody rather than to think or try.

Why should they work so hard when the lead singer doesn't have a care in the world? Some may make the excuse that they don't know how. Perhaps others will blame someone else for their shortcomings.

"It is what it is" echoed throughout the first company we discussed at the beginning of this book. I would love to tell you that the company thrived despite the mass spell those words had conjured, but unfortunately, the company did fold. Nothing is achieved when everyone has the attitude that "it is what it is."

Change your station. Yes, you can do that. In fact, you are the *only* one who can change the way you think and your actions. Find new ways of doing things and get moving to bring about the changes you want to see.

As we conclude this chapter, let's reflect on the journey we've embarked upon and the strides we've made. In the tapestry of life, resilience, determination, and unwavering resolve come together to create a masterpiece that defies the pied piper's call to give up. Remember the saying about the great oak being a little nut that held its ground; likewise, we are reminded that even from small seeds of courage, mighty possibilities can grow.

Defying the Pied Piper's Call

Pamela's story is one of courage and love. Faced with a tough diagnosis, she refused to give up in whispered tunes of surrender. Instead, she composed her melody of strength, leaving behind precious memories for her children, a symphony of love that will echo through generations.

Then, we shift to a team bonded by tenacity and determination, a living embodiment of the spirit that defies the piper's call. As challenges arise, they don't succumb to the melody but rally under the banner of Mr. Murphy's Law, foreseeing and outsmarting obstacles with ingenious solutions. They show that obstacles, though inevitable, can be overcome with determination and creative thinking.

In this grand symphony of resilience, Pamela's story harmonizes with the team's endeavors, forming a chorus that echoes the same resolute message. The piper's call to resignation can be silenced, and in its place, melodies of unwavering perseverance can rise. Pamela's choice to embrace life's moments and the team's determination to overcome hurdles are both narratives that illuminate a path that leads away from the piper's tempting path of least resistance.

It Is What It Is

Let's remember that the refrain "it is what it is" need not dictate our fate. Instead, let Pamela's legacy and the team's accomplishments serve as a counterpoint, a resounding call to action, urging us to stand firm and take charge of our narratives. Let us choose to rewrite the melodies of our lives, harmonizing with the chords of courage, resilience, and unyielding determination. The allure of the pied piper may persist, but its spell can be broken by the triumphant melodies of those who refuse to surrender to its tune.

Think about a recent mistake or failure in your life. How might approaching yourself with self-compassion rather than self-criticism shift your emotional response and support your growth?

What support systems or resources can you draw upon when facing difficult decisions or circumstances?

Chapter Seven

Empower Your Journey

It Is What It Is

We often navigate through life, flipping through its pages without truly absorbing its richness, and only a few of us actively seek to enhance it. However, resisting the temptation to merely trudge through each day in a monotonous march is essential. Remember, you are unique, and every interaction, no matter how small, leaves an impact on those around you. As Ronald Reagan, the actor-turned-fortieth president of the United States, once said, "Every new day brings with it possibilities." It's within your power to recognize and seize these opportunities.

One morning, I watched an interview featuring Amanda Gorman. For those unfamiliar, Amanda Gorman, born in 1998 in Los Angeles, California, faced challenges due to an auditory processing disorder that affected her pronunciation of the letter *R*. Turning to poetry as a means of coping, she rose to prominence, becoming the first National Youth Poet Laureate in 2017 while attending Harvard University. Amanda Gorman is among the few who have had the honor of reciting a poem at a US presidential inauguration.

During the interview, a reporter asked Miss Gorman about her approach to reading a book. Her response brought a smile to my face and echoed a sentiment we should all embrace in life. Amanda reads a book once to enjoy it, then revisits it a second time to absorb its essence, and finally, on the third read, she contemplates how she could enhance it. Amanda's ability to perceive numerous possibilities within a book surpasses what many people may discover in a lifetime. She elevates her now-what? moments to a higher realm.

You are surrounded by people every day. Make it a point to surround yourself with positive, like-minded individuals. Just like the old saying, steel sharpens steel, you want to be surrounded by people who keep you sharp, not dull. Find the ones that foster a physically and mentally healthy way of life. Your friends and family may help determine who you are and possibly may be the driving force of your future. Even when you think your future is bleak, remember there are very few things in this life that other people haven't gone through. You get to choose how you define your journey.

Consider the remarkable story of Kayla McKeon, born with Down syndrome. When Kayla was little, she told her mother and father that someday she would drive a car. Kayla's mother and father didn't just smile and pat her on the head, thinking she would never be able to drive a car. Instead, they told her of the things she must do to be able to drive, including that she must be able to read to get a driver's license. This motivated Kayla to become a voracious reader. When Kayla got older, she earned her driver's license not on the first try but on the fifth. Kayla is one of the few with Down syndrome to do so. She could have easily accepted failure the first time she took the test, but I don't think the word *failure* is in Kayla's vocabulary. I believe in the power of language and how we choose our wording, and I think Kayla saw the first four attempts as knowledge gained and a denial of the license until she was ready for the responsibility.

At thirteen, Kayla began training and competing with the Special Olympics New York. She competed in several sports, including bocce, soccer, and floor hockey. Kayla won bronze and silver medals in the 2011 Special Olympic World Games. As a floor hockey goalie, she may have denied the other teams many a goal, but for Kayla, it was all about helping people. Her passion transcended driving and sports when she entered politics. Kayla is the first lobbyist on Capitol Hill with Down syndrome. She created a podcast called *Kayla's Corner*, where she discusses Down syndrome and her viewpoint of DC politics. Kayla would not have been able to achieve any of this if she was not surrounded by positive, reassuring family and friends.

Positivity can also help reduce stress and improve finances. Look at the study of Dr. Martin Seligman from the University of Pennsylvania, where he studied sales professionals. Of two groups, he found the more positive group outsold the glass-is-half-empty salespeople by 56 percent. In addition, more optimistic people are usually happier and have fewer frown lines. So, let's keep our glasses half full, shall we?

In addition to positivity, it's helpful to also reevaluate yourself consistently. Knowing your strengths, you will be more confident and easily apply them, which may also leave you more time to strengthen your weaknesses, because you are focusing on what is important to you and what prospect you may want to explore. For example, just as I understood as a young manager that I lacked understanding of myself and others, I took it upon myself to become a better version of myself by learning those things. This led me to be more effective in getting the things I wanted to achieve.

Remember Kayla? She has a humbling attitude. If she needs help, she asks for it, and she is always ready and willing to help others, always an optimist. You should be humble enough to ask for help or ask for someone else's perspective. There is so much information in this rapidly changing world that no one person could know and understand everything, let alone *do* everything. By talking with other people, you will gain their wisdom, knowledge, and understanding of how they view their world. The pied piper would have us believe there is no great future, but you know better. The future is there for us to explore and learn it, then to write it. You have learned to look for the now what? and strive for the future you desire and deserve. Envision what you want. Implement a plan and achieve it, just like Kayla.

Many people say, "I can't see myself owning my own business" or "I can't see myself amassing enough money to retire at fifty-five." When you have this mindset, you limit yourself. For example, until 1954, it was believed that no human could run a mile in fewer than four minutes. We can thank Roger

Bannister for breaking that barrier. In Oxford, England, at the age of twenty-five, Roger ran a three-minute, 59.4 second race. Once people saw it could be done, hundreds did it. It's the same as in any other sport: Once someone breaks a record or does something seemingly impossible, others follow.

In the tapestry of life, we're constantly surrounded by people who shape our journey. It's crucial to deliberately seek out positive, like-minded individuals who uplift and inspire us. Seek out those who not only promote physical well-being but also nurture mental health. Our circle of friends and family often plays a significant role in shaping who we are and can be a driving force in shaping our future. Even during moments of despair, remember that others have faced similar challenges. It's all about how we choose to define our journey.

By engaging with others, we gain valuable wisdom, knowledge, and diverse perspectives, enriching our understanding of the world.

You need to see yourself fulfilling a role or achieving your goal. That is why, in 2016, SeeHer was started. Its mission is to portray all women and girls accurately in marketing, advertising, media, and entertainment so they see themselves being there and doing the thing that they thought only their male counterparts could achieve.

If a little girl can't imagine becoming president someday, she won't even try. If a young lady cannot visualize herself as a music producer, she won't become one. SeeHer understands that if she can see herself in someone, she can *become* her. We hear more and more about breaking the glass ceiling or being the first to be in that position. Once that has been accomplished, it throws open the doors for others to flood in, just like in athletics once records are broken and people see it can be done. But without realizing that you can do it or be it, you are unaware of the possibilities.

I learned this early in life. My brother opened my eyes and mind to see the different possibilities laid before me. One of the first games that my brother taught me was checkers, which is an excellent game to teach children. It builds their confidence and helps them create strategies. Checkers teaches you to make decisions, implement actions, and make judgment calls.

For one year, my brother and I went to the same school, and at the lunch hour, when we were done with our meal, we could do anything with that remaining free time. My brother could always be found playing checkers with someone. I can remember him resembling the bronze sculpture of Auguste Rodin's *The Thinker*; he would sit at the table with his hand on his chin and his other arm across his knee, plotting his next move as his opponent nonchalantly slid a checker across the squares. His first rule was that if a player removed their finger from the checker, their move was over. My brother was quirky in that he always had a large paper clip he had unfolded as a pointer. When it was his time to move a checker of his choice, he placed the tip of the uncurled paper clip to the farthest ridge of his chosen checker, and he would slide the checker to a position. Then, he would ponder his opponent's next move and counter his move without moving his paper clip.

I often saw him slide the checker back to its original position. Then, he contemplated keeping the paper clip on the checker and then moving the checker to the new square, repeating the process of thinking about what his opponent would do. With his survey of the board, he was then satisfied; he flicked the paper clip up off the checker like a maestro would start the beginning of a great symphony, then with three jumps, he landed at the other end of the board and received his king's crown.

His second rule was that players must always jump. As you remember, he is eight years older than me. As you can imagine, there were many times that I did not see the possibility of jumping his piece, but in return, he would capture mine for *not* taking the jump. The most frustrating times were when multiple moves would involve overtaking his pieces. If I did not see two jumps, I would lose my checker. The worst was when two different checkers could make jumps. I could only jump one, which I would be allowed to do, removing his checkers from the board, but then I lost my other piece for not moving two checkers at once. In life, you should always try to envision possible moves. Then, when it's time for you to jump, you can jump with increased confidence.

Of course, sometimes, no matter how hard you try, you will feel as if you have failed, but be assured no learning experience should be chalked up as a failure. The only way we can truly learn is by trial and error. Failure is part of life. The only actual failure is not trying. If you get defeated, stop and analyze why. Try not to make the same mistake twice and remember it is commonly said that insanity is doing the same thing repeatedly and expecting a different result. When this happens, stop yourself and take a step back, look at what is happening, and make the needed corrections.

You saw this with Pamela. She faced the fact that she would no longer be around for Tom and the kids. She looked at the possible moves that Tom and the kids would take in the future, and she made sure she would be part of their lives even if she was physically unable to be there herself. Remember when Kimberly asked everyone into the conference room, and we essentially laid out the metaphorical checkerboard, looking at all the possible moves we had to make to finish the project? When Kayla told her parents that someday, she would get a driver's license, she meant it. It may have taken her five tries, but she did it.

We interact with our coworkers, family members, and people we encounter by chance. So, take the time to look at your daily gameboard, stop and ponder the possibilities, remember that every action you take will have a reaction, and make your move accordingly. The only way to move forward and win this crazy game of life is to play. If the pied piper leads you, or anyone around you, to be drawn to "it is what it is," be sure to pose the question, "Now what?" Then, plan your next move. See yourself doing it, then make a plan of action and achieve it. You are in this game to win.

As the curtain falls on this chapter of your journey, remember that life isn't meant to be merely skimmed through like the pages of a magazine. It's a vibrant tapestry of opportunities and challenges waiting for you to immerse yourself fully.

Ronald Reagan once reminded us that every day begins with untapped possibilities. It's these very possibilities that Amanda Gordon so skillfully uncovers in the stories she reads, reminding us to read not just with our eyes but with our hearts and minds, allowing the now-what? moments to elevate us.

Surrounding yourself with positivity and like-minded individuals isn't a choice but a necessity. Just as Kayla McKeon found strength and achievement within a supportive network, so can you. Embrace humility, seek guidance, and learn from the wisdom of others. Every interaction is a chance to learn and grow and to gather insights that expand your understanding of the world.

Positivity isn't just a mindset; it's a key to thriving. Dr. Martin Seligman's study resonates with the power of optimism, showing that it not only brightens your outlook but can also influence your success. Your strengths are your allies, your weaknesses are your opportunities for growth. Strive to be a better version of yourself every day, just as Kayla did on her journey to driving success.

But remember, envisioning your goals isn't enough. It is as important to see the possible moves ahead, just like a game of checkers. Your plans may need adjustment, and your path may be strewn with challenges, but every move teaches you something invaluable. Failure is a stepping stone toward success, for each attempt brings wisdom and insight.

The tales of Amanda, Kayla, and the remarkable people who break barriers remind us that limitations are often self-imposed. The barriers you shatter today inspire countless others to follow suit. The mission of SeeHer exemplifies the power of representation, where visualization becomes realization. Just as Roger Bannister made the impossible possible, so can you redefine the limits of your potential.

As you navigate this intricate game of life, remember the lessons from the checkerboard. Be thoughtful and deliberate in your moves, for every decision sets in motion a chain of events. The symphony of your journey is composed of your choices, tenacity, and unyielding belief in yourself.

In this grand game, you are both the player and the architect. Embrace each day with the question, "Now what?" and embark on your path with purpose. The pied piper's tune may linger, but let it only serve as a reminder of the path you choose not to tread. With every interaction, every decision, and every leap, you have the power to craft your victory.

So, as the game continues and the future beckons, play with intention, passion, and resilience. Your journey is yours to empower, embrace opportunities, make strategic moves, and ultimately claim victory in life's extraordinary game.

Explore the concept of active listening as a foundational skill for building authentic connections. How can practicing more attentive listening and genuine curiosity enhance your ability to connect with others on a deeper level?

In moments of doubt or hesitation, how can you harness the power of your own determination to push forward, even when the odds seem stacked against you?

Chapter Eight

Never Limit Yourself or Others

It Is What It Is

Comedian Chad Daniels tells a joke about his son possibly being a super genius. He said to his son once that the sky is the limit, and his son replied, "I don't understand why people say that when there are footprints on the moon." The takeaway from this is that people have a tendency to put limits on us when the reality is there are no limits, just the ones we let others or ourselves put on us. You should always strive to be a better you, and a better you will attempt to aspire to the ones around you, not settle for being just average.

This chapter will address ways to help others be more mindful and take responsibility for their actions. How would you feel helping others achieve greater heights?

Once upon a time, there lived a magnificent golden mare named Honey. She ran wild and free among the meadows of flowers. The legend was that you would know when Honey was near, for the pounding of her hooves could be felt in your heart when she would approach. However, Honey was not alone, for she had a little colt. Honey named him Remo, which meant the strong one, but Remo felt he was anything but that. He did not feel as powerful and surefooted as Honey, and his coat was not as golden as the sun or the flowers in the fields. It was, in fact, a coat of late evening dusk.

One day, Honey and Remo were walking among the grasses of the Grand Prairie. Honey told Remo to eat the grass if he wanted to be big and strong and have a beautiful coat like hers. Remo sniffed the grass, took his hoof, and pawed at the ground but did not eat the grass as his mother commanded. He thought nothing would help him grow big and strong, especially grass. At that moment, Remo felt a little paw touching his leg. He looked down at a curious looking little animal peering up at him.

Finally, Remo asked, "What are you?"

"I am a prairie dog, and my name is Ellie!"

Ellie put one paw on her hip and with the other one, gestured to the prairie and said, "I guess you haven't gotten around to tasting any of the beautiful grasses and flowers of this lovely prairie?"

Remo said, "No, I'm not hungry."

"What a shame," Ellie said. "There are so many different grasses on this prairie, all with their unique flavors. Take these two, for instance; if you take a bite of this plant with its big dark green leaves, you'll find it tastes peppery, and if you grab a chunk of the short bright green grass, you'll taste how sweet it is."

So, Remo leaned down and took a tiny nibble of the dark peppery leaves. Then, he lifted his head to the sky, contorted his mouth to the left, closed one eye, and turned his head to the right as he chewed.

"Peppery," Remo said.

Then he took a big mouthful of the bright green grass, and his eyes lit up. "Oh my, that *is* sweet," Remo said.

As the weeks and months went by, Remo tried every grass and flower available to him. He would even recommend different grasses for Ellie to try.

One afternoon, Remo and Ellie were near a stream, and Ellie said, "I bet you couldn't have imagined when your mother said to eat up all the yummy grasses in the field that you would become so big and strong and grow such a beautiful coat."

Remo looked inquisitively at his little friend Ellie.

"What do you mean?"

Ellie smiled and said, "Just look at yourself in the reflection of the stream."

Remo looked down at his reflection in the water; looking back at him was a stallion the color of beautiful glistening coal.

Remo's mother told him directly to eat the grass to grow big and strong, but Ellie used her words differently to achieve the same desired outcome. Never underestimate how your words will shape the future for better or worse. As parents, teachers, managers, and even friends, the words you choose and how you use them will have an extraordinary power to affect the people around you.

Think of the people around you like an orchestra, and you are the conductor. Conducting is an art form. The conductor directs from the center, gesturing with head, arm, hand, and even finger movements and facial expressions that unite the performers, setting a tempo and executing precise beats. In addition, the conductor listens and uses critical thinking to shape the orchestra's sound so that each instrument is heard as the composer intended.

You are likely thinking some form of *I'm not head of a company; I'm just an average Joe; how am I supposed to be a conductor?* That's a fair enough question.

It Is What It Is

Check out Dave and Jason at the age of sixteen. They both got after-school jobs at one of the local car dealerships. They started at just two hours a day during the week. They were supposed to sweep the floors and take out all the trash. They found the job relatively easy and would finish all the tasks within two hours. This is where the two young men differed. Jason followed the pied piper. He enjoyed strolling along the aisles of shiny new cars and imagining himself flying down the road in one or spending time playing with others in the back, throwing and kicking a giant tape ball they had made.

On the other hand, Dave used his time differently. He was not fond of the pied piper; he strove to do more, be more, and achieve more. It started with small tasks. When he was done sweeping and taking out the trash, he asked the parts manager if he would like him to break down the empty boxes and throw them in the recycling bin. The parts manager appreciated Dave taking the initiative in helping out and encouraged this work ethic in different ways. When summer vacation came around, the dealership manager asked both boys if they would like to increase their hours for the summer. Dave and Jason both showed up the next day at 7:00 a.m. but were given quite different jobs. Jason was expected to do all the sweeping, take out all the trash, and break down all the boxes in the recycling bin. Dave was asked to become a porter. Some of his responsibilities included driving the new cars to their appointed spots on the lot, and when customers dropped off their vehicles to be serviced, he would drive them back to the service bays. As the years went by, Dave became one of the most successful salespeople at the dealership. He always told the new part-time kids how he started out sweeping floors, but because of his initiative and his own now-what? mentality, he didn't stay there. His time working as a porter, parts manager, and getting into sales exemplified the natural progression that is expected from hard work and a vision of the future.

He always ended his conversation with those young men and women with the biggest smile as he unlocked his shiny red car and told them, "I was once just like you, sweeping floors and dreaming of fast cars. Don't take your eyes off the prize; one day, you will have yourselves a shiny red car, too."

When Dave got his first job sweeping floors, he didn't know he would end up being a salesperson, let alone the best salesperson at the dealership, but Dave always took pride in what he did and always looked for other things to do. This work ethic did not go unnoticed and opened many doors for him. Dave didn't settle for simply being a part in the orchestra, he took it upon himself to become the conductor of his own life.

As we draw near the conclusion of this narrative, let's pause to reflect on the journey. In the vast symphony of life, we often find ourselves dancing to the tunes of others, swayed by the melodies of their expectations and limitations. But the story of Remo and Ellie reminds us that words and actions have great power and can shape destinies, transform doubts into strengths, and turn ordinary moments into extraordinary accomplishments.

Chad Daniels's comedic anecdote about his son's innocent insight echoes with profound truth. The notion of the sky is the limit fades in comparison to the indelible footprints on the moon. It's a reminder that the boundaries we often accept are merely illusions, products of our hesitation or others' attempts to define us. The journey to become a better version of ourselves requires breaking free from these self-imposed limitations.

Consider the tale of Remo and Ellie. Through Ellie's guidance and Remo's willingness to try, the colt blossomed into a magnificent stallion with a coat as dark as midnight. Ellie's choice of words and nuances of encouragement led Remo to unlock his hidden potential. This narrative teaches us that the *way* we communicate with and support others can be the catalyst for their growth and transformation.

Picture yourself as the conductor of an orchestra, guiding the intricate blend of instruments to create a harmonious masterpiece. Your words and actions shape the symphony of people and their work around you, setting the tempo for success, growth, and empowerment. Just as a conductor listens attentively to each instrument, adjusting and fine tuning, you too have the power to listen, guide, and elevate those around you.

You might think, *But I'm not a CEO or a leader.* However, the story of Dave and Jason underscores that every role holds potential. Dave didn't simply settle; he became the conductor of his own life's orchestra.

So, how do you become the conductor of your life? It starts with embracing the now-what? moments that cross your path. These moments are invitations to rise above complacency, challenge the status quo, and steer your journey in a direction aligned with your aspirations. Just as Dave saw potential in every role he took on, you too can seize opportunities to create a transformative narrative.

As you conduct your life's symphony, remember that your influence extends beyond yourself. Like Ellie guiding Remo, your words can inspire, your actions can elevate, and your belief in others can propel them to heights they never thought possible. Your ability to see the untapped potential in those around you is a gift, one that can change lives and shape destinies.

So, let the tale of Remo and Ellie resonate within you. Embrace your role as the conductor of your journey and the lives you touch. Be deliberate with your words, guide with intention, and orchestrate a harmonious narrative where limits fade, potential soars, and each crescendo of success is a testament to the power of your influence.

The future beckons and the conductor's baton is in your hands. The symphony of your life is waiting to be composed. What will be your next move? How will you shape the melodies of your story and those around you? As you take the stage of life, remember that the limit is not the sky but the expanse of your imagination and determination.

Consider the power of language in shaping beliefs and behaviors. Are there any phrases or expressions you commonly use that may inadvertently reinforce limiting beliefs or expectations?

What lessons can be drawn from the prairie dog's method of communication in terms of fostering growth and learning in others?

Chapter Nine

Stay on Target

The score is tied. The quarterback catches the snap, and he takes three steps back. He sees his receiver. He throws the ball, and his receiver catches it and runs it to the goal unopposed. The crowd is going wild. The home team has won. *It is what it is!*

Yes, sometimes "it is what it is" means just that. The game has been won. It is over. It's in the history books. Let's think about this for a moment. For the team that won, there was nothing more they could do. They achieved their goal, which was to win the game. However, the team that lost must look at the "now what?" The loss of that game may have put them out of the playoffs, causing them to reflect on their season and where their strengths and weaknesses were. The coaching staff likely spent hours, days, or even weeks looking at what plays worked and which ones didn't, and figuring out how to improve their team and game for the next season. Theirs didn't end with "it is what it is," but instead provoked the thoughtful "now what?" which must be explored.

I am a certified shooting coach under USA Shooting and 4-H Shooting Sports. When I coach someone to shoot in a competition, I teach them it is crucial to be mindful of each shot. What I mean by this is during a shooting competition, participants fire sixty shots with a possible score of 600. The goal, of course, is to have each shot in the center of the target hitting a score of ten each time. As I coach an individual, I remind them to be mindful of the shot they are presently taking. I encourage them to not think about the shot they've already taken because it is history. Time after time, a shooter will throw a shot, meaning it is far from the desired score. They end up hitting a five, and all they can think of is *I cannot hit another five. If I hit another five, it's going to be awful. No more fives.* So what's their next shot? It's usually a five.

Time and again, you will see the imagery of staying on target or reaching your goals by seeing an archery bull's-eye with several arrows piercing the target rings. Let's look at the 4-H discipline of archery and see what we can take from the simple act of drawing back the bowstring and hitting our target, which can be a great metaphor as it correlates with our personal goals. To launch the arrow forward toward the target, you must first draw back the bowstring. By doing so, the outer wheels of the compound bow will multiply the force applied to the bowstring, giving you a more significant mechanical advantage for storing potential energy. This gives you the ability to relax and concentrate on the target. In other words, sometimes, you need to step back before moving forward. Taking that step back, just like drawing the bowstring back, will sometimes allow you to think and multiply your thoughts and strategies, which will compound your momentum forward to enable you to relax and concentrate on hitting your target and achieving your goals.

It's valuable to remember the past. That's how we learn, but you don't want to obsess over the past because it will keep you there. You don't want to be stuck in regret or anxiety over something you cannot change. It's best to deal with it and put it to bed so that you can move on. When shooting in a competition, one person has the highest score; however, you are still the winner if you can match or exceed your personal best.

I once worked with a 4-H group of first-time shooters as young as eight years old. It was Olivia's first time shooting an air rifle. The first or the second shot didn't even hit the paper. I saw that she was quickly getting upset. I knew her problem was that she was not looking at the sites properly. She ignored the rear sight and only looked at the front sight, a common challenge for first-time shooters. I took out a pen and paper and drew what she needed to be looking for. The third shot ripped right through the paper! Olivia started to get excited, as she began to understand. The fourth shot broke into the rings and was within scoring. There was improvement with each shot. I asked Olivia to take a deep breath and relax. I asked her to imagine the pellet splitting the paper in the black center rings.

As she squeezed the trigger back and we heard the pop of the pellet hitting the target, I yelled out, "You hit in the black. It's an eight!"

She was ecstatic with excitement. She shot four more targets, and at the end of the class, I laid all five out in concession and took a picture. You could see she started so far off target, but by that fifth target, not only were all five shots within scoring, they were all in the black. Olivia's mother pulled me to the side in the last week of classes. She told me that Olivia had tried other sports but was never very good at them and got very discouraged before she saw any improvement. Learning the sport of shooting encouraged her to strive to do her personal best each time she pulled the trigger.

It Is What It Is

Olivia could have stopped after the first target and allowed her frustration to overcome her and convince her that she couldn't do it. Instead, she saw immediate improvement once she took a little guidance and saw further improvement with practice. That year, on her Christmas wish list was an air rifle. Yes, she did get that rifle, and as she gets older, maybe we'll see her at the Olympics.

I was watching a baseball game; the batter came up to the plate and swung at the first pitch. The umpire called strike one. The baseball player literally hit himself in the head, struck the ground with his bat, and then kicked the ground with his foot. He then got back in the batters' box. The batter was still visually upset with himself, shaking his head and talking to himself. I turned to my husband and said he was stuck in his head. It was apparent to everyone that all he could think about was how he was messing up, and of course, he kept striking out. He could not get past himself to move forward.

Did you know that the best way to trap a monkey is to hollow out a small opening in a gourd just big enough for a monkey to put his hand in? All you do is weigh this hollow gourd down with sand and then put a tasty treat inside the gourd. When the monkey puts his hand in the gourd and grasps the treat, he is trapped because he is so focused on not letting go of the prize. He has formed a fist around it that will not allow his hand to slip out of the hole. The only reason he is trapped is that he won't let go of the treat. If he lets go, he is free.

"Now what?" The monkey can put his hand back in and become trapped again, walk away without the treat, or he could tip the gourd over and pour out his treat with the sand.

It doesn't matter where you are in your life. What is important is how you conduct yourself. Take pride in what you do, see things for how they are, and don't stumble over the lies that are told to you or the lies you tell yourself. See the possibilities. Don't let fear stop you from grabbing what you want. Surround yourself with people that will make you stronger. Recognize that the only thing holding you back will then be you. Stop and take the time to look at the situation no matter what. Seek out the possibilities; there are usually more than one. Be willing to set your pride to the side. Yes, it will be scary and hard work, but that's life. Get out there and live the best life you can, and when you hear that old pied piper sing, "It is what it is," you will be able to answer him by belting out, "Now what?"! And you will stop him in his tracks when you show him what you're capable of doing.

As we come to the close of this chapter, let's reflect on the power of resilience and determination in navigating life's challenges.

In life, as in sports, I've learned that the power of mindfulness can transform outcomes. Just as dwelling on a missed shot leads to more misfires, fixating on the past traps us in a cycle of regret. Instead, we must take a deep breath, draw back the bowstring, and focus on hitting the target. Sometimes, this allows us to gather our thoughts, multiply our strategies, and compound our momentum toward success.

The story of Olivia, the young shooter aiming for excellence, resonates. Her journey began with frustration, but rather than succumbing to self-doubt, she chose to learn, grow, and strive for her personal best. Olivia's tale underscores a truth: Progress requires moving forward, guided by a mindset unburdened by past setbacks.

Imagine the monkey and how he remains trapped by his stubborn grip on a prize, unable to let go. How often do we let our limiting beliefs and fears ensnare us, keeping us from embracing new opportunities? Like the monkey, our freedom lies in releasing what no longer serves us, relinquishing the grip on old narratives, and daring to leap into the unknown.

As the pied piper sings, "It is what it is," we *do* have a choice. We can echo that sentiment and remain passive, or we can interrupt the melody with a resounding "now what?" This challenge to the status quo awakens our potential. We are the conductors of our lives, orchestrating our journeys with purpose, intention, and a refusal to be confined by circumstances.

Reflect on a time when you allowed fear or self-doubt to hold you back from pursuing your goals. How can you cultivate the courage to overcome those barriers and take decisive action?

In what areas of your life do you find yourself getting stuck in the mindset of "it is what it is"? How can you challenge that mindset and adopt a more proactive now-what? approach?

Conclusion

It Is What It Is

As our time reaches its finale, let the wisdom we've uncovered be your guiding light. Just as the pied piper's tune tempts us to accept the status quo with "it is what it is," let us boldly respond with "Now what?" Remember that life's journey is an intricate dance of choices and opportunities. Each now-what? moment is a chance to change the rhythm, to rewrite the narrative, and to shatter the limitations that the melody may place upon us. Embrace the transformative power of these moments. The quarterback's throw, the archer's draw, and the shooter's focus all teach us that the present is where we act, where we shape the future. So, my friend, let's stride forward with purpose. Let's challenge the tune with our melodies of growth, resilience, and empowerment. When we hear "it is what it is," let our resounding response be a triumphant "now what?" And through this, let's journey forth, not as mere observers but as conductors of our own stories, crafting symphonies of possibility and triumph in the face of the unknown.

The final chapter may be written, but your story is far from over. The pen is in your hand; the next chapter awaits.

About the Author

Suzanne Slovak's career began in her family's wedding business, where she gained first-hand experience as a printer and photographer. Her journey continued in St. Louis, where she honed her craft in special effects slides before embracing large-format printing. Eventually, she moved into management, overseeing operations for 15 years. Today, Suzanne has pivoted to sales, fueled by her fascination with human behavior and team dynamics. This book encapsulates her insights on leadership, offering practical strategies for motivating oneself and others to embrace change, critical thinking and lead with integrity and inspiration.

SSlovak.com

info@sslovak.com

For more great books from Empower Press
Visit Books.GracePointPublishing.com

PEAK PRESS

If you enjoyed reading *It Is What It Is,* and purchased it through an online retailer, please return to the site and write a review to help others find the book.